Genealogy Made Easy

Introduction

Genealogy is the fascinating world of tracing your family name back into a time once lost. It can either be an enjoyable past time or at times quite frustrating. It can tell you about some great dark secret that had been lost to time or even about some lost hero in your family tree.

I have been working on my family tree for approximately 25 years and back in the early days when I had just started out researching my genealogy line, I wish I had known what I know now. In this book, I will be giving you some ideas on how to start your own family tree, as this is one of the most asked questions any new genealogist asks. I also want to go into some information on where to start looking for information and searchable links. So if you have not started a family tree before, this book will help you get started and if you are already working on your family tree, maybe there is some link that you didn't know about to knock down a wall or two. So come on along with me and lets dive into your past.

Content

OK, So what is a family Tree and why is it so important to record it....

A family tree in it's basic form is a group of people connected through blood and marriage. Parents, cousins, wives, husbands, children, they are all connected by different branches, in the shape of a tree like form. It starts with you, and works up the trunk towards your parents and then on to their parents and your other relatives and branching out back through the centuries and ages.
The importance of researching your family tree is to be able to tell your future generations how they are connected to vast, interlocking families. It can reveal who you really are and why you have a certain eye colour, skin tone, personality etc etc. If doing a family tree didn't really matter, why do people bother to spend a lot of time taking photographs of family members to pass down to the next generation. And the oldest family tree is in the pages of the bible. My best advice to you, is start your family tree (genealogy line) while you are young, before family members die and those memories are lost forever.

First things first,

Lets cover what you are going to need for starting your own family tree.

A basic kits should contain several pens, lead pencils, a rubber and a couple A4 binder exercise books with a minimum of 96 or 128 pages.

Why you should have these main items for the basic kit...

Pens: Well, get used to doing a lots of writing, when researching your tree, you will be taking notes from family members eg: grandparents, parents, aunties or uncles etc and it is easier to read pen written notes later than it is using pencils and you can't always take notes on a computer or phone.

Pencils: There are going to be times when you have to use a pencil. Like in research centers, libraries and some other places where they frown upon people using pens as they don't wish the documents to get damaged.

A rubber: for rubbing out mistakes.

A4 Binder books: There is going to be a lot of loose pieces of paper with notes on, if you get into practice writing the notes in a binder book. The notes wont get lost and then when the book is full; if you keep them in a folder they can be at easy reach, for later on. Also one book can be used each family name.

Here are some Do's and Don't's to help you to remember while working on your family tree.

Always try and get full names of family members and try to get the possible correct spelling. This will make your research a lot easier.

Don't abbreavate any location or name because who ever takes on your work in the future won't know if you mean this place or that place.

Don't just think inside the box. - I mean your name may be spelt one way now, but in years gone by the spelling may vary a little. so check all versions of the name.

Double check everything in case of mistakes made online. There will be a lot of people with the same names as your relatives but they may have different parents or siblings or even married someone else.

Now that you have your basic kit, you are ready to start your family tree.

Take one of your exercise books and make a list of everyone you know of and can remember, including yourself. This will be a reference for you to go back to many times, ticking the ones you have spoken to about your family tree information.

If you look at it this way, you will start with YOU, write down your full name and date of birth and where you were born. Then you will work backwards to your parents and then on to their parents and so forth.

If you follow my checklist this will help you get started...

This is probably one of the most important things to do first. Why, because accidents can happen and while you are spending time looking for photos etc people die and then their memory of something is lost and most times when you are talking to family members about the family tree, they tend to bring out the photographs anyway.

Talk to your relatives, they will know stuff.

Ask your parents, grandparents, aunts and uncles about their memories and if your grandparents are already dead what they remember of their parents and grandparents.

Don't ask just about birth and death facts get any other dates too, also get any of the stories they can remember hearing when they were growing up. Try to phrase questions with.. when, why, where, how and what.

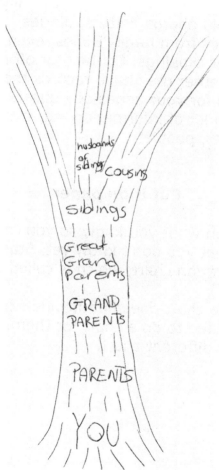

As you can see from the diagram, very quickly your tree will growing.

Gather what you already know about your family tree

Scour your attic, closets or basement, or your family members to collect family records, old photos, letters, diaries, photocopies from family Bibles, even newspaper clippings. Contact far off relatives to ask whether they have records that may be of help for your genealogy quest. Photo's can hold a lot of information, eg; clothing, erea places, people.

Put it on paper

Write down what you know so you can decide what you don't know yet. Start with a five generation chart, which is called a "pedigree".
A pedigree chart does not include siblings, so if you wanted to do a chart for them. each one has a different chart.

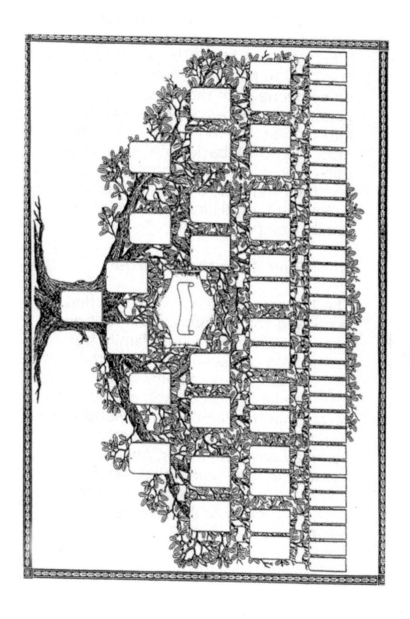

Focus on your research

Where are the blanks in your family tree? Don't try to fill them in all at once, focus on someone from the most recent generation where your chart is missing information. Try to answer that "mystery" first, then work backwards in time. And don't worry too much about your siblings and their families, they will be added when you put this information into a family tree program.

Searching the Internet

The Internet is a terrific place to find leads and shared information, but don't expect to find your whole family tree online. You can search many of the biggest databases of names on the web with one or two clicks. You can search records on the Familysearch website for free for some basic info and other ones you may have to pay for. Ancestry subscribers can search that site from home, or see if your local library offers Ancestry Library Edition for free on its computers.

Explore Websites

Once you've searched for the last names in your family, try websites specifically about your ethnic heritage or parts of the country where your relatives may have lived. You may even find websites about your family created by distant relatives researching the same family names and trees.

Discover your local FamilySearch Center

The Church of Jesus Christ of Latter-day Saints has more than 4,000 FamilySearch Centers where anyone can tap into the world's largest collection of genealogical information. Using your local center, you can borrow microfilm of records such as the birth, marriage or death certificates of your ancestors. More than 2 million rolls of microfilmed records from all over the world are available. Compare the information in these sources with what you already know; fill in the blanks in your family tree, and look for clues to more answers to the puzzles of your past.

Plan your next step

Once you've exhausted your family sources, the internet and the libraries you may want to travel to places your ancestors lived, to visit courthouses, churches, cemeteries and other places where old records are kept. This is also a rewarding way to walk in the footsteps of your ancestors and bring your heritage to life. You'll find that the quest to discover where you came from is fun and many mysteries are just around the next corner and as exciting as a detective story, and it is never-ending.

Organize your new information

Enter your findings of your family tree into a genealogy program or on paper charts (make sure you note your sources). File photocopies and notes you have collected from family members, photographs or source so you can refer to them again.
There are a number of genealogy programs on the market, and we will look at some here. I have used in the past "Legacy Family Tree" and I am currently using Ancestry Family Tree Maker, mainly because I like the chart Kinship, which tells me; how all my realitives are related to me.

Here are some other Genealogy programs available.

Roots Magic
https://www.rootsmagic.com/
Enter an unlimited number of facts, notes, sources, and multimedia items to each person and family. It makes it easy to track multiple relationships such as adoptions, foster parents, and more. Import directly from Family Tree Maker, PAF, Legacy, The Master Genealogist, and Family Origins. Plus RootsMagic Essentials has full GEDCOM 5.5 support for both import and export.

Ancestral Quest
http://www.ancquest.com/
Easy data entry, keyboard shortcuts, scrapbooking, and excellent sourcing capabilities are just some of this genealogy software program's wonderful award-winning features. Create professional looking Pedigree Charts, Family Group Sheets, Ancestry charts, Descendant charts, genealogy book reports, fan charts and more.

Legacy Family Tree
http://www.legacyfamilytree.com/
has 25 charts and 20 reports, it also links to Familysearch and Ancestry.com. but it doesnt have web hints. It imports & exports via a Gedcom file.

Family Tree Heritage

http://www.familytreeheritage.biz/

Family Tree Heritage brings you powerful yet easy-to-use features to help you tell your family story. Searching for ancestors and creating your tree is just clicks away! Find records and important documents by searching the world's largest genealogy database.

My Heritage

https://www.myheritage.com

Millions of families around the world use MyHeritage to explore their history. Collaborate with members and join the thousands who reunite with long-lost relatives every single day through our network. Research your family history with three award-winning products, all private and secure. Sync between them and enjoy a captivating journey to your past, wherever you are.

Brother's Keeper

http://www.bkwin.org/

Brother's Keeper is a Windows genealogy program that will help you input and organize your family history information and let you print a large variety of charts and reports. Brother's Keeper works with Windows 98, ME, NT, 2000, XP, Vista, Windows 7, 8, 8.1, and Windows 10.

Heredis

https://www.Heredis-online.com/
Search for your ancestors in *350 millions* shared family trees posted online by Heredis Online users.

Family Historian

http://www.family-historian.co.uk/
Family Historian 6 is the latest version of the powerful, award-winning genealogy program with comprehensive features designed to meet the needs of the beginner and expert alike. Try Family Historian free for 30 days. After 30 days you must purchase a license, and be assigned a registration key, to continue using the program.

Family Tree maker

http://www.mackiev.com/ftm/
Quickly and easily build your family tree and Update your tree on the go with Tree Sync to Enhance your tree with charts, reports, photos, and more. View family history timelines and interactive maps. Includes free 14-day trial subscription to Ancestry.com

As you can see there is quite alot of programs to choose from.

Links to Searchable sites

In this section I will be giving you a list of links which may help you in your search of family names, I have found these site over the years and I still use them in my quests.

Cornwall online parishes
http://www.cornwall-opc-database.org/
Here you can research cornwall's BDM records and sometimes it has maps too.

UK Census Online
http://www.ukcensusonline.com/
Search census records from 1841 - 1911, has some free search options with further costs to see full records.

The church of Latter day saint research centre
https://familysearch.org/
With a FamilySearch account, a world of family history possibilities comes to life. Start making connections today.

Free searching the UK for BDM
https://www.freebmd.org.uk/
FreeBMD is an ongoing project, the aim of which is to transcribe the Civil Registration index of births, marriages and deaths for England and Wales, and to provide free Internet access to the transcribed records.

UK Links

Cornwall parishes etc
http://www.cornwall.gov.uk/community-and-living/parish-and-town-councils/
Town and county parishes

Newspaper clippings for UK and World
http://newspaperarchive.com/
from 1607 - 2016, there is a 7 day trial for 2.16+ billion newspaper articles. 6 month membership of $49.95 Australian.

Scotlands People
www.scotlandspeople.gov.uk/
Searches for BDM, parish records for Scotland, has basic searches plus fee searches for further seeing records.

Who were the Covenanters
www.covenanter.org.uk/WhoWere/
Scottish Covenanter Memorials Association

Gloucestershire, Bristol Marriage Index 1644-1939
www.findmypast.com.au
The records include 12,138 marriages from St. Mary Redcliffe Church, which is the tallest building in Bristol.

Gloucestershire, Bristol Baptism Index 1660-1914
www.findmypast.com
Explore more than 400,000 names in this
baptism index from Bristol. The index includes
110 parishes.

More Bristol Records
http://forebears.io/england/gloucestershire/
bristol

London Map 1877
mapco.net/parish/parish.htm
Showing parishes and boundries

London Records
www.london.anglican.org
London parishes

www.forebears.co.uk/
View parish registers from 1535 to 1925
online

Kent, England Online Parish Clerks
www.kent-opc.org/
Kent Online Parish Clerks who provide free
family history, genealogy information and
record transcripts for your personal research.

Middlesex England Parish Records
http://www.angelfire.com/fl/Sumter/
Middlesex.html
The database is for parish marriage records in
Middlesex County, England between 1563 and
1895. Parishes covered are:- Acton, Ashford,
Cowley, Ealing, Edmonton, Enfield, Feltham,
and more.

Mid Kent Marriage Index - Mid-Kent Marriages
Index 1754-1911
www.woodchurchancestry.org.uk/
midkentmarriages/
All parishes and all years from 1754 to 1911
are included.

Lancashire Births Marriages & Deaths Indexes
www.lancashirebmd.org.uk/
The Register Offices in the county of
Lancashire, England, hold the original records
of births, marriages and deaths back to the
start of civil registration in 1837.

Huntingdonshire Genealogy Resources &
Parish Registers
forebears.io/england/huntingdonshire
Huntingdonshire Cemeteries. Deceased Online
(1629-Present).

Yorkshire BMD
www.yorkshirebmd.org.uk/
Yorkshire County Births, Marriage and Deaths
Indexes.

Cambridgeshire Family History Society
https://www.cfhs.org.uk/
Family history within the old counties of
Cambridgeshire and the Isle of Ely.

The Domesday Book Online - Derbyshire Home
www.domesdaybook.co.uk/derbyshire.html
Domesday place-names and landowners

Derbyshire Marriages 1538 - 1837
www.derbysmarriages1538-1837.co.uk/
Online index contains over 75,000 marriages

Lancashire Census
lancashirecensus.co.uk/
Lancashire Census data from 1841-1901

Staffordshire Parish Registers Society
www.sprs.org.uk/
Information about the Staffordshire Parish
Registers Society

Staffordshire Births Marriages & Deaths
Indexes
www.staffordshirebmd.org.uk/

Northamptonshire parish registers & parish records
ukga.org/Registers/northamptonshire.html
A collection of complete Parish Register transcripts and Phillimore marriages for the county of Northamptonshire - free to view online.

Warwickshire Online Parish Clerks
www.hunimex.com/warwick/opc/opc.html
Data may include census, parish registers

Devon Parish Registers Online
www.devon.gov.uk/pronline.htm
Original parish registers for much of Devon

Sussex Online Parish Clerks
www.sussex-opc.org/

Parish registers & Online
www.knightroots.co.uk/parishes.htm
Hampshire Online Parish Clerk

Isle of Wight Family History Society
www.isle-of-wight-fhs.co.uk > Databases

Leicestershire Parish Registers
leicestershire.webs.com/

United Kingdom & Ireland - England
www.cyndislist.com
FreeBMD Marriage Index: 1837-1915

Lincolnshire
https://www.lincstothepast.com/
View Lincolnshire related images

Lincolnshire Marriage Indexes 1837-1850
mi.lincolnshiremarriages.org.uk/
Lincolnshire Marriage Indexes

Cheshire Births Marriages & Deaths Indexes
www.cheshirebmd.org.uk/
Cheshire County Births, Marriage and Deaths
Indexes

Norfolk Family History Society Parish
www.norfolkfhs.org.uk/indexes,parish-
register-transcripts/

Nottinghamshire Family History Society
www.nottsfhs.org.uk/

Oxfordshire Family History Society
www.ofhs.org.uk/

RUTLAND Genealogy Records
www.familytreecircles.com/
surname_RUTLAND.html

Shropshire Family History Research
www.shropshirefamilyhistory.co.uk/

Somerset Family History Research Service
www.britishancestors.com/research/
somerset.php

Sheffield City Council
https://www.sheffield.gov.uk/libraries/
archives.../family-history/south-yorkshire.html

Doncaster and District Family History Society
doncasterfhs.co.uk/

British Army WW1 Service Records, 1914-1920
www.greatwar.co.uk/research/...records/
british-soldiers-ww1-service-records.htm

Search WW1 Service Records
www.forces-war-records.co.uk/

British Army soldiers after 1913
www.nationalarchives.gov.uk

Australian Links

British Convict Transportation Registers Database
www.slq.qld.gov.au/resources/family-history/convicts
The British Convict transportation registers 1787-1867 database has been compiled from the British Home Office.

NSW Convicts
https://www.records.nsw.gov.au/archives/collections-and-research/guides-and-indexes/convicts
searchable database containing certificates of freedom; bank accounts; deaths; exemptions from Government Labor; pardons; tickets of leave; and, tickets of leave passports. There are 140,000+ entries.

More Western Australian Convicts
http://members.iinet.net.au/~perthdps/convicts/con-wa.html

Tasmanian Archives Online
search.archives.tas.gov.au/
Search catalogue provides descriptions of State and local government and private records including files, letters, manuscripts, maps, plans

First Fleet Convicts Register
firstfleet.thruhere.net/
Convict Names, Sex, Occupation, Age when
departed England etc.

Convict Records of Australia
www.convictrecords.com.au/
search the British Convict transportation
register for convicts transported to Australia
between 1787-1867.

National Library of Australia
https://trove.nla.gov.au/
online searches for photos, books and newspaper
clippings

First Fleet - Searching
firstfleet.uow.edu.au/search.html
contains a searchable database of 780 First
Fleet convicts

Tasmanian BDM
www.justice.tas.gov.au
The following records are available online at
the Tasmanian Archive

Western Australian Convicts
http://www.sro.wa.gov.au/archive-collection/
collection/convict-records

Army – World War I
www.naa.gov.au

Online Database Search - Genealogy SA
https://www.genealogysa.org.au/resources/
online-databases.html

Adelaide Cemeteries Authority > Records
www.aca.sa.gov.au/Records

Cemeteries - Naracoorte Lucindale Council
https://www.naracoortelucindale.sa.gov.au/
cemeteries

Graham Jaunay - South Australian Council
Cemeteries
www.jaunay.com/councilcems.html

Australian Cemeteries - South Australia
www.australiancemeteries.com.au/sa/

South Australian Cemeteries - Family History
South Australia
www.familyhistorysa.info > australia > sa >
bmd's

Irish Links

Records of 49,000 Irish WWI dead in new digital archive
www.irishtimes.com

Finding records for Irish soldiers involved in WW1
www.irishcentral.com

Ireland's World War 1 Veterans 1914-1918
www.worldwar1veterans.com/

Welcome to Irish Genealogy
https://www.irishgenealogy.ie/

Irish Family History Online Records Search facility
https://www.rootsireland.ie/

Order Irish Births Deaths Marriages Online
https://www.birthsdeathsmarriages.ie/

Catholic Parish Registers
registers.nli.ie/

400,000 parish records online
www.irishcentral.com

Public Record Office of Northern Ireland
https://www.nidirect.gov.uk/proni

Emerald Ancestors, Northern Ireland
Genealogy & Ulster Ancestry
https://www.emeraldancestors.com/
Free search of over 1 million Northern Irish
Birth, Marriage, Death & Census records

General Register Office for Northern Ireland
https://www.gov.uk/general-register-office-
for-northern-ireland

Irish Famine Immigrants, 1846-1851
findmypast.co.uk
www.findmypast.com.au/...records/...records/
.../irish-famine-immigrants-1846-1851

Emigration Records (Ireland) - GenGuide
https://www.genguide.co.uk/source/
emigration-records-ireland/170/

North American Links

The Famine Immigrants
www.lalley.com/famine.htm
Lists of Irish Immigrants Arriving at the Port of New York

Free Ships' Passenger Lists to USA, Canada, England, Australia
www.olivetreegenealogy.com/ships/

Immigration Records | National Archives
https://www.archives.gov/research/immigration

TheShipsList: Passengers, Ships, Shipwrecks
www.theshipslist.com/

Passenger and Immigration Lists Index, 1500s-1900s - Free ...
www.ancestralfindings.com/cd354.htm
Database contains listings of approximately 2750000 individuals who arrived in United States ports between 1538 and 1940.

Soldiers and Sailors Database - The Civil War (U.S. National Park ...
https://www.nps.gov/civilwar/soldiers-and-sailors-database.htm
The Civil War Soldiers and Sailors System

New Zealand Links

BDM Online - Department of Internal Affairs
https://www.bdmonline.dia.govt.nz/

New Zealand Birth, Death and Marriage
Historical Records
https://
www.bdmhistoricalrecords.dia.govt.nz/

Papers Past - National Library of New Zealand
https://paperspast.natlib.govt.nz/

Obituaries from Papers Past- New Zealand
Bound - Freepages
freepages.genealogy.rootsweb.ancestry.com/
~nzbound/obits.htm

New Zealand : Newspaper Archives & Indexes
: History : Internet ...
christchurchcitylibraries.com

Other Online Family Tree Sites

Genes Reunited: Discover your ancestors
www.genesreunited.com.au/
Discover your family history online today with
Genes Reunited. Find your ancestors and
create your own family tree online.
Membership is approx $20 for 6 months

Family Tree Searcher: Family Trees Searched
at Eleven Sites
www.familytreesearcher.com/
Search family trees at eleven online sites by
entering ancestor information once.

Trace your Family Tree Online | Genealogy &
Ancestry
www.findmypast.com.au/
Trace your ancestry and build a family tree by
researching extensive birth records, census
data, obituaries and more with Findmypast.

Family Tree Templates
https://www.familytreetemplates.net/
These printable blank family trees and
ancestor charts are perfect for genealogy
research and class projects.

Family Echo - Free Online Family Tree Maker
www.familyecho.com/
Draw your printable family tree online. Free
and easy to use, no login required. Add photos
and share with your family. Import/export
GEDCOM files.

Australia Ship Passenger List Ancestor
Searches
www.searchforancestors.com › Free Genealogy
Records
begin your genealogy search here with the
best collection of Australian ship passenger
lists database searches. Find your ancestry &
build a family tree.

Glossary

Gedcom - is an acronym standing for Genealogical Data Communication.

Pedigree - A pedigree chart is a tool for genetic or genealogical research

Maternal grandfather - is a person's mothers father

Paternal grandfather - the father of someone's father

First cousins - people in your family who have two of the same grandparents as you, in other words, they are the children of your aunts and uncles.

Second cousins - shared a great-grandparent: Your **second cousin** is the grandchild of your great aunt or great uncle.

Third cousins - shared great-great-grandparents: Your third **cousin** is the great-grandchild of your great-great uncle or great-great aunt.

Fourth, and Fifth Cousins: fourth cousins have the same great-great-great-grandparents, and so on.

Removed - You and your first **cousins** are in the same generation (two generations younger than your grandparents), so the word "**removed**" is not used to describe your relationship. The words "**once removed**" **mean** that there is a difference of one generation. For example, your mother's first **cousin** is your first **cousin, once removed**.

Second cousin once removed - is the child of your second cousin.

First cousin twice removed - is the grandchild of your first cousin.

Notes